# אבאבאבאבאבאבא
# CRAFTS
## OF THE ANCIENT WORLD

# THE CRAFTS AND CULTURE OF
# THE ANCIENT HEBREWS

## Joann Jovinelly and Jason Netelkos

the rosen publishing group's
rosen
central

*To Allison*

Published in 2002 by The Rosen Publishing Group, Inc.
29 East 21st Street, New York, NY 10010

First Edition

## Library of Congress Cataloging-in-Publication Data

Jovinelly, Joann.
The crafts and culture of the ancient Hebrews / Joann Jovinelly and Jason Netelkos.
p. cm. — (Crafts of the Ancient World)
Includes bibliographical references and index.
Summary: Describes easy-to-make crafts that replicate the arts of the ancient Hebrews.
Includes historical material, a timeline, a glossary, and resources.
ISBN 0-8239-3511-6
1. Jews—Civilization—Juvenile literature. 2. Jews—Material culture—Juvenile literature.
3. Creative activities and seat work—Juvenile literature. 4. Handicraft—Juvenile literature.
[1. Jews—Civilization. 2. Handicraft.] I. Title. II. Series.
DS112 .J685 2002
933—dc21
                                                                    2001004952

*Manufactured in the United States of America*

**Note to Parents**
Some of these projects require tools or materials that can be dangerous if used improperly. Adult supervision will be necessary when projects require the use of a craft knife, an oven, a stovetop, plaster of paris, or pins and needles. Before starting any of the projects in this book, you may want to cover your work area with newspaper or plastic. In addition, we recommend using a piece of thick cardboard to protect surfaces while cutting with craft or mat knives. Parents, we encourage you to discuss safety with your children and note in advance which projects may require your supervision.

# CONTENTS

## THE CULTURE

## THE CRAFTS

Most of what historians, scholars, and scientists know about the ancient Hebrews is based entirely on information that is contained in the Bible. And while many people believe that the Bible is a factual document—the word of God recorded faithfully by his followers —other people believe that the Bible was conceived and written by ordinary men and that it represents the traditions, myths, communal memories, and beliefs of the Israelite people. Like many other documents from the ancient world, the stories contained in the Bible were probably passed from generation to generation orally (through storytelling and public worship) and then, centuries later, put into writing. It is difficult to gauge the Bible's accuracy, no matter what your personal beliefs. But it does tell us a great deal about the Hebrew people and what life must have been like for them. Other

*This wood engraving depicts Abraham journeying into the land of Canaan.*

information about the culture of the Hebrews comes directly from scientists and archaeologists who have studied surviving artifacts from the period.

According to the Hebrew Bible, Israelites traced their ancestry to the nomadic shepherd Abraham. He was said to have been chosen by God to lead his household northward from Sumeria, a kingdom in southern Mesopotamia (which borders the Persian Gulf and present-day Saudi Arabia), to Canaan, a land by the Mediterranean Sea just east of Egypt. In return for his devotion, God told Abraham that he and some of his descendants would be granted the land of Canaan as an inheritance.

Abraham and his people wandered throughout the lands of Canaan and into Egypt and back, similar to many nomadic tribes of the time that traveled from place to place in search of adequate food and water. Most likely, Abraham and his followers rode donkeys and lived in fabric tents. They also traveled with flocks of sheep and goats, like many modern-day shepherds still do in the Middle East.

Abraham's grandson Jacob had twelve sons. Jacob's name was changed to Israel and his descendants became known as the Israelites. According to information in the Hebrew Bible, the Israelites left Canaan around 1700 BC because of a widespread famine there. They settled in Egypt, an area that was ruled at the time by the Hyksos, Asian invaders who had entered Egypt around 1650 BC. The Israelites were allowed to settle in Egypt and remained there for 400 years, increasing in number and prospering, just as God was said to have promised Abraham.

One of the central stories in the Hebrew Bible concerns a defining event that followed this period of prosperity—the Israelites' exodus (departure) from Egypt. As the Egyptians regained control of their land from the Hyksos, whom they had enslaved by 1315 BC, a new dynasty of powerful, wealthy pharaohs came to power. One of these pharaohs—possibly Ramses II (who reigned from 1279 to 1212 BC)—feared the growing strength of the prospering

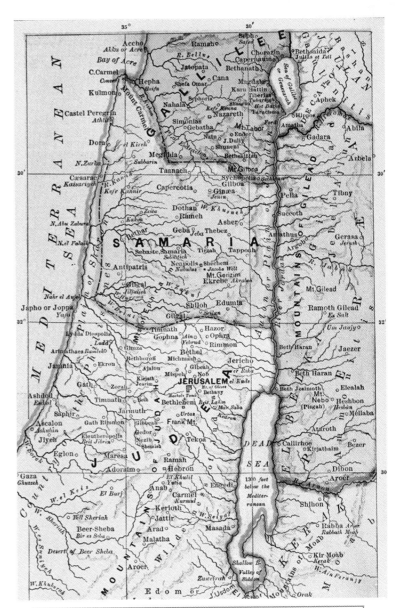

*This map illustrates the lands inhabited by the Hebrews in biblical times.*

Israelites and believed that they would eventually turn against Egypt and conquer the lands so recently won back from the Hyksos. The pharaoh wanted to prevent this by reducing the Israelites' power and numbers, so he ordered that they, like the Hyksos, be enslaved. In addition, he made it a law

*This illustration shows the pharaoh's daughter finding the infant Moses.*

the pharaoh to let his people leave Egypt peacefully to resettle in their promised land: Canaan. When Moses' request was denied, God unleashed great hardships on the people of Egypt, including a series of ten plagues. The Nile River was said to have turned into a stream of blood symbolizing all the Hebrew infants who had died in its water. Further plagues included deadly weather (hail), infestations (frogs and locusts), and three days of absolute darkness. The final plague came in the form of an angel of death who killed the firstborn sons of all Egyptian families. At this point, the pharaoh relented; the Israelites were free to go.

The story of the exodus mentions that, as the Israelites fled Egypt, the Red Sea parted, allowing them to escape the pharaoh's army. With walls of water piled up on either side of them, Moses and his followers walked on a dry path across the seabed and into the Arabian Desert.

The Torah, or the laws of the Jews, was given to Moses by God atop Mount Sinai. The two tablets Moses brought down with him became known as the Ten Commandments. In truth, however, there were many more laws that made up the Torah. All of these laws or guidelines that were delivered to Moses by God were meant to help his people live a

that all male Hebrew infants born during his reign be drowned at birth. The Bible tells the story of one such infant, placed in a basket and set down upon the waters of the Nile by his mother and sister who hoped to save his life. The baby was found by the pharaoh's daughter. She adopted the child and named him Moses. He was then raised as an Egyptian prince.

After learning as a young man that he was a Hebrew and not an Egyptian, Moses became a leader of the enslaved Israelites and tried to convince good, moral life. The followers of Moses, over a million people according to biblical accounts, were expected to make a promise to uphold those laws. The agreement of Moses' followers to obey the Torah was called a covenant. In return, God promised the Israelites the land of Canaan and eternal protection.

On their way to Canaan, the Israelites were disobedient to both God and Moses. Some even worshiped a golden calf. They were punished by being forced to wander in the desert for forty years before reaching the Promised Land. Just before crossing into Canaan, Moses died. A strong man named Joshua took his place and led the Hebrews into their new home. Eventually, after King Solomon's reign, the nation split. Ten tribes formed Israel in the north, and two formed Judah in the South.

# POLITICS AND WAR

The twelve tribes had leaders, or kings, called *shoftim*. They were expected to uphold the word of God. Their duties also called for them to defend their newly occupied land from the Philistines, people from Greece who had earlier invaded the same area. Because the Israelites had no official leader and no centralized army, however, fighting the Philistines was a difficult task.

One of the most famous leaders of Israel, David, became king in 1004 BC. He defeated the Philistines and entered the city of Jerusalem, where he built a palace for himself and planned for the construction of a monumental temple to God that would house the Ark of the Covenant, a holy chest that housed the Ten Commandments. By David's death and the end of his reign in 965 BC, Jerusalem had developed into a large, highly developed cultural center that stretched from Mesopotamia to the Dead Sea. David's son, Solomon, became the next king of the Israelites, and it was he who helped the city develop further by extending trade routes and agreements with many surrounding nations, including Syria, Arabia, and Egypt. He also enlisted as many as 30,000 servants to construct the temple David had planned but didn't live to see built.

Many years later, in 722 BC, when Israel was invaded by Assyria, the Hebrews fled their homeland and again found themselves wandering in exile at the mercy of foreign hosts. Later, Nebuchadnezzar, king of Babylonia, conquered and enslaved the Hebrews of Judah. He destroyed the temple and the entire city of Jerusalem. The exile of the Jews from their homeland to foreign lands became known as the Diaspora, or dispersion of the Jewish people.

*Israelites celebrate the rebuilding of Solomon's Temple in Jerusalem.*

Enslaved and exiled, the Hebrew people began their quest to regain the Promised Land. They got the chance in 539 BC, when Babylonia was overthrown by Cyrus, the king of Persia. Cyrus wanted to rebuild the land of Judah and offered the Hebrews materials and money to salvage the lands they had lost and to rebuild their sacred temple.

It was not long, however, before the Greeks gained strength and eclipsed the power and influence of Persia.

Alexander the Great and his mighty soldiers swept through Egypt, Judah, Syria, and India, capturing those lands and its people and forging the Greek Empire. This era is known as the Hellenistic period, a time of great prosperity and peace for Jews who adopted Greek ways, but a dark period of persecution for those who clung to old forms of worship. An even more repressive empire was about to sweep over Israel, however, imposing its own social order, religion, and culture. By 63 BC, the Romans had seized nearly all of the Mediterranean, including Greece and Judah, which became known by its Latin name, Judea.

All of the civil unrest that followed in the wake of the Roman conquest divided the Jewish people. Some wanted to follow the Romans and their laws, while others wanted complete religious and political freedom. These people became known as zealots (a word we still use to describe people with strong, even fanatical, convictions). In defense of their beliefs, these zealots killed many Roman soldiers. The fighting continued, and as many as 100,000 Jews were crucified as punishment, including a wandering preacher named Jesus whom the Romans feared was encouraging the Hebrews to rebel. Finally, when the Roman leader Florus had offended the Jews by sacrificing blemished animals inside their temple—

an action that violated religious law—outraged Jews stormed the sacred building and killed him. As word of the event quickly spread, war between the Jews and Romans escalated, leaving Jerusalem in complete chaos and the temple burned to the ground. In a final move, the Romans changed the name of the nation from Judea to Palestine.

*This relief panel is from the inner facing of the Arch of Titus in Rome. It depicts the Romans looting Solomon's Temple.*

## DAILY LIFE

The earliest Hebrew people, probably because of their nomadic existence, received little formal education and were less accomplished in crafts like metalwork and pottery than other, more settled and stable civilizations. Like all nomads, they were tent dwellers and established a more permanent system of housing only after the founding of Israel and Judea. They lived off the land, herded sheep and cattle, and traveled on the backs of donkeys. They were constantly on the move as the climate changed from season to season and the arid desert became even drier and less hospitable. Some Hebrews became tradesmen and carried spices and other goods from Egypt to Syria.

When the Hebrews finally did settle in permanent communities, all activity was centered near the home. The family normally consisted of three generations and was ruled by the father. Some archaeological findings indicate that a typical Hebrew home was a three- or four-room mud brick structure with a second-story area for sleeping. It had a clay roof that

*This is an ancient Hebrew coin.*

was supported by several cross beams. Many of these homes also had open courtyards where, during the summer months, women laundered clothing and cooked over an open fire.

Home life was busy, with women doing most of the chores and men either herding the sheep and cattle or making their living as merchants. Women were financially dependent on their husbands, and children were expected to respect their parents. If a childless woman's husband died, his brother was expected to marry her in order to produce children to continue the family line. It was a common custom for men to have many wives, but a woman could have only one husband. Divorce,

if it was granted, could be obtained only by a man.

Education was conducted at home in the form of structured activities that were often led by the mother of the household. The emphasis was on teaching religious tradition and beliefs as well as community values. In addition, boys would often be instructed in a trade while girls learned domestic skills. It was only after the Jews established themselves in Israel and Judah that male children were taught by scholars and teachers in synagogue schools. Like the Egyptian and Roman civilizations, the Hebrews educated a team of young men to act as scribes—literate men who would draw up contracts, keep accounts, and maintain records. Scribes were also expected to be of high moral character.

# LANGUAGE

The development of the Hebrew language can be divided into three distinct periods: biblical or classical Hebrew (in which most of the Hebrew Bible was written), Mishnaic or Rabbinic Hebrew (beginning around AD 200 and bearing the influence of Babylonian and Syrian languages), and the modern Hebrew language of today. The earliest forms of the language are more than 3,500 years old and originally resembled Egyptian hieroglyphs. Most of the time, scribes were the only common people who had a complete understanding of the Hebrew characters, which were heavily influenced in their design by ancient Aramaic.

The earliest Hebrews wrote on wet clay tablets with a wedge-shaped stylus that carved glyphs into the tablet's surface. Later, they used papyrus—just as the Egyptians did—and another kind of paper called parchment. Like the Greeks, Hebrews would also occasionally write on fragments of broken pottery. All of the writing was formed in ink (with the exception of the clay tablet carvings).

# ART

Because it was against religious law to create images of God or any idols, the Hebrew people left behind very little traditional art in the form of sculptures or paintings. They did, however, create many objects from clay, such as food containers and oil lamps, and decorative items such as jewelry. Many other cultures that they came into contact with through trade and during their periods of exile and conquest, such as the ancient Egyptians, Greeks, Arabs, and Romans, influenced the artistic sensibilities of the Hebrew people.

One of the most artistically rich eras in the history of the Hebrew people was during the Hellenistic period (332 BC to AD 30), a time of high art and learning for both the Greek and Jewish cultures. The ancient Egyptian city of Alexandria (founded by Alexander the Great) became a Jewish center of learning, and many Hebrews prospered there after arriving as immigrants when Judah was invaded by conquerors. The Alexandrian Hebrew community flourished so much that Jewish scholars translated the Hebrew Bible, or Tanakh, into Greek. One famous story claims that seventy Jewish scholars each translated the Tanakh into Greek and that every one of those translations was identical. This was taken as a sign that God's hand had intervened in the sacred labor. The translation became known as the Septuagint (Latin for "seventy," the number of translators). Because of this translation, many Greek-speaking nonbelievers converted to Judaism.

Alexandria remained a vibrant, intellectual city until the Romans conquered the Greek Empire in AD 63.

# Art and Architecture

Although Solomon's Temple no longer exists, the Hebrew Bible locates it in the ancient city of Jerusalem. The construction of Herod's Temple, which was designed to cover the remains of Solomon's Temple in the first century BC, destroyed the original building's foundation and masonry. Even earlier, Babylonian invaders ransacked the temple in 586 BC and stole its treasures, leaving the only remaining evidence of its existence contained within biblical descriptions of it.

King David, who had brought the Ark of the Covenant to Jerusalem and wanted to build a worthy sanctuary in which to house it, ordered the construction of the temple but died before it was built (the Bible says that God wanted his temple built by David's son, Solomon, because David had killed too many men in war). Solomon began the work in the fourth year of his reign and completed it seven years later with the help of Phoenician craftsmen and indentured servants (workers bound by contract). Phoenicians lived along the

*Servants and laborers help cut cedars for Solomon's Temple.*

Mediterranean Sea north of Canaan. It is said that the stones used to construct the temple were carved, shaped, and decorated at the quarry so that the temple area itself was free of the noise of hammers, axes, or any other tool.

*The Wailing Wall in Jerusalem is the only remaining wall of a temple complex built by Herod the Great.*

Considered one of the most impressive houses of worship in the ancient world, Solomon's Temple was a lavish building with an inner sanctuary where the Ark of the Covenant was kept. The walls of the house (the area outside the inner sanctuary) were made of cedar and carved with images of gourds, palm trees, angels, and flowers. The ceiling was also made of beams and planks of cedar, while the floor was made of cypress. The walls of the inner sanctuary and its altar were also made of cedar. Doors to the house and the inner sanctuary were made of olive wood and carved with the same images that adorned the walls. No stone could be seen within the temple; it was all covered with wood. Once all of these wood planks and beams were in place, the walls, ceiling, floor, doors, and altar were covered with pure gold and semiprecious stones.

Today, the only known relic that still exists from the original temple is a small ivory pomegranate, believed to be a decorative element that once resided within its walls.

*This is a model of Solomon's Temple at the Holyland Hotel in Jerusalem, Israel.*

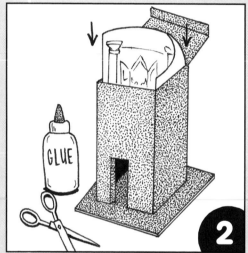

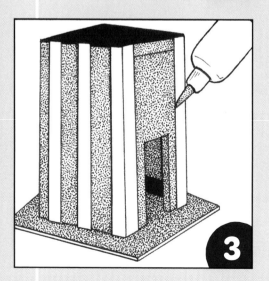

# Solomon's Temple

*Over the centuries, many artists have tried to depict the lost Solomon's Temple. Now, you can create your own imaginary version of this mysterious, ancient wonder.*

### YOU WILL NEED
- A small rectangular box
- Cardboard scraps
- Masking tape
- Glue
- Scissors
- Markers or crayons
- Craft paint

### Step 1
Draw a picture of the inside of your temple on a piece of paper, slightly smaller than your box. Perhaps draw palm trees, flowers, and gourds to echo the wood carvings thought to decorate the original temple's walls. Color your picture with markers or paint.

### Step 2
Draw a rectangular doorway on your box and cut it out with scissors. Insert your drawing from the top of the box and glue it in place. Glue the bottom of your box to a piece of cardboard as a base.

### Step 3
Cut narrow strips of cardboard of equal width to make at least ten columns. The columns should be of equal height and no taller than the box itself. Glue them around the length of the box, equally separated, as shown.

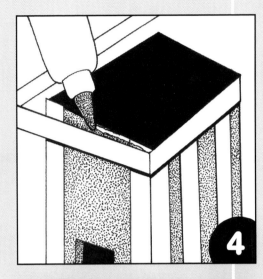

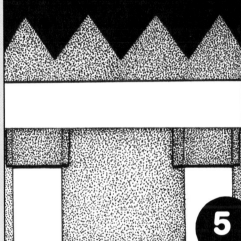

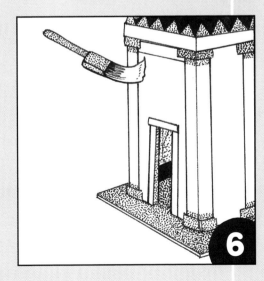

### Step 4
Glue a cardboard strip around the entire area of the top inch of the box.

### Step 5
Add details using pieces of cut cardboard and attaching them to the box with glue. Cut a strip of cardboard into a zigzag to decorate the roof.

### Step 6
When the glue on your temple construction is completely dry, paint the outside walls and columns in any color you desire.

# Religion and Beliefs

According to the Hebrew Bible, Moses was commanded to construct the Ark of the Covenant—a gold-covered wooden chest—as a sacred storage vessel for the tablets containing the Ten Commandments. The materials to be used to build it—acacia wood, gold, silver, brass, onyx, linen, and ram's hide—and its size and shape were said to be dictated by God.

*The Ark of the Covenant was carried around Jericho before trumpet blasts brought down the city's walls.*

The ark was placed in the Holy of Holies (the most sacred place in the temple, where the divine presence was felt). The Hebrew Bible states that the ark was beautifully carved and topped with two cherubim, or angels, with outstretched wings. It was housed in the inner sanctuary, called the Holy of Holies, in Solomon's Temple. This sacred room could be entered only by the Kohen Gadol (a high priest) during high holy days such as Yom Kippur (the Jewish Day of Atonement).

The Hebrews carried the ark with them into battle, believing that it ensured victory, and looked to it for strength and guidance when traveling in exile through the barren desert lands of Arabia. For them, it served as a focal point of worship when they were without homes or temples. During these periods of exile, the ark was housed in a tent, called the tabernacle. Though homeless, hungry, and wandering, the Israelites could always look to this tent and feel reassured that their God traveled with them.

Yet the ark, according to several passages in the Bible, was as dangerous as it was sustaining. Some people were said to have been struck dead after making inappropriate offerings to the ark, and another story claims that an escort of the ark was killed instantly when he reached out to steady it as it wobbled upon a moving cart. The Bible states that foreign enemies who captured the ark for themselves and their nations in battle became afflicted afterward with terrible diseases such as leprosy and plague. Until they returned the ark to the Hebrews, their sacred plunder would continue to bring them only death and destruction.

The Bible states that the ark disappeared from Solomon's Temple forever in 586 BC, when the Babylonians invaded Jerusalem. Some believe that the ark is still buried beneath the temple ruins, inside an underground cave.

*This painting depicts the fall of Jerusalem and the start of Baylonian captivity.*

*This is an artist's rendering of the Ark of the Covenant.*

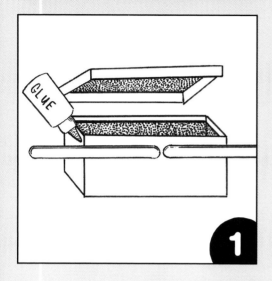

# The Ark of the Covenant

*Decorate this box and use it as a container for your own spiritual books or personal writings.*

### YOU WILL NEED
- Small cardboard box with lid
- Popsicle sticks
- String
- White glue
- Newspaper
- Modeling clay
- Craft paint

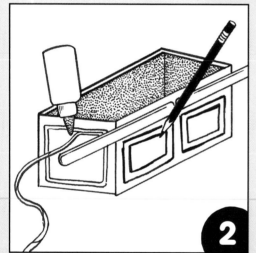

### Step 1
Before decorating the ark, remove the lid and set it aside. Glue two Popsicle sticks to each side of the box for handles, as shown.

### Step 2
Draw simple designs on your ark with a pencil. Trace your pencil lines with a continuous bead of white glue, covering small sections at a time. Drape the string over the lines of glue.

### Step 3
To make angels for the top of your ark, roll a quarter-sized piece of modeling clay in your hand; this will be the angel's torso. Next, roll two pieces of clay of equal length into tube shapes; these will serve as the angel's legs. Then roll a small ball for the angel's head. Join the head, torso, and legs as shown. Make a set of wings by cutting small triangular pieces of cardboard and inserting them into the clay body. Repeat steps to make the second angel in the same manner. Set them facing each other on the top of the ark's lid.

## Step 4
Rip newspaper into small pieces and dip them into watered down white glue (three parts glue to one part water) to make a papier-mâché paste. Cover the clay angels and the entire lid of the box with three to four layers of wet newspaper strips. Allow it to dry overnight.

## Step 5
Once the lid is dry, you can decorate the sides of it in the same manner as the ark itself, drawing a design and then covering it with glued string. Decorate the angels with fringed paper gowns. Cut arms from thin cardboard and glue them in place.

## Step 6
Paint the entire ark and its lid with craft paint, in colors of your choice.

# Writing and Literature

Hebrew is just one of the Semitic languages of the Middle East. Still, many Israelites adopted other languages for both speaking and writing, such as Greek, Arabic, Aramaic, and, much later in the nineteenth and twentieth centuries AD, Yiddish (a combination of old Hebrew, old German, and Slavic languages), French, Russian, Spanish, Ladino (a mixture of Spanish and Hebrew), and English.

Historically, there were two sets of Hebrew alphabets: the early Hebrew and the classical, or square, Hebrew, neither of which contained any vowels. Early Hebrew—similar to Egyptian hieroglyphs—had twenty-seven picture characters and is more than 3,500 years old. By the sixth century BC, however, the square version of the alphabet was more common, and it was shortened to just twenty-two letters. Hebrew would change yet again over the next 1,500 years, though much less radically, and begin to resemble the modern Hebrew that is still in use today.

Outside of the Hebrew Bible, one of the most revered texts of the ancient world is the Dead Sea Scrolls (a collection of Scripture fragments, named after the cliff-side cave by the Dead Sea in which the scrolls were found). The cave and scrolls were discovered in 1947 by several young shepherds who were searching for a lost goat in the Judean desert. Upon entering the cave, the men

*This Hebrew passage from the Book of Genesis relates an episode in the life of Joseph, a young Hebrew who was sold into slavery in Egypt.*

*These are fragments of the Dead Sea Scrolls.*

came upon a series of clay jars that were filled with scrolls that appeared to be ancient.

According to both linguists and scientists (who used a method of dating artifacts called carbon-14 dating), it is estimated that the scrolls were written between the third century BC and AD 68. Evidence from the scrolls themselves indicates that they were written by scribes in Qumran, a settlement on the edge of the Dead Sea of which a complex of ruins still remains.

Since the initial discoveries, the Dead Sea Scrolls have become a subject of great speculation by both historians and the general public. Who lived in Qumran? What sort of settlement was it? Who placed the scrolls in the cave? Why did they do so? A small group of scholars have been poring over the scrolls since soon after their discovery, but very little information concerning them has been released publicly. We can only hope answers to these tantalizing questions will eventually be provided.

*A Bedouin shepherd found the first seven Dead Sea Scrolls in two jars.*

*A Torah Scroll of the kind found in many synagogues.*

# Ancient Scroll

*Write beautiful Hebrew characters on this homemade "ancient" scroll.*

### YOU WILL NEED
- 2 cardboard paper tubes
- Cardboard
- Coffee can
- Pencil and scissors
- Plastic straws
- Masking tape
- White glue
- Brown paper bag
- Craft paint
- Scrap paper
- Black paint or markers
- Paintbrush, if desired

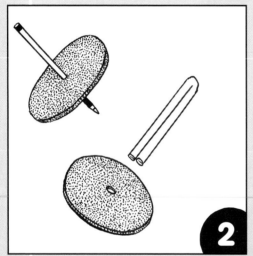

### Step 1
Trace the bottom of a coffee can onto a piece of cardboard four times. Cut the four circles out with scissors.

### Step 2
Carefully puncture a hole into the center of each circle. Fold a straw in half and stick both ends into the hole of each circle. Tape securely on the reverse side. These will be the handles of your scroll.

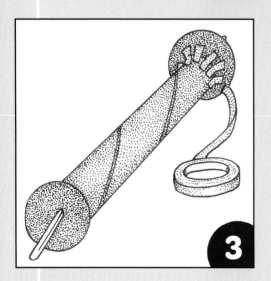

### Step 3
Tape each circle to the ends of the cardboard tubes, as shown. Use craft paint to paint the handles.

### Step 4
Cut open a paper bag along the seam and unfold it into a large sheet with an 11-inch width. This will be your writing surface.

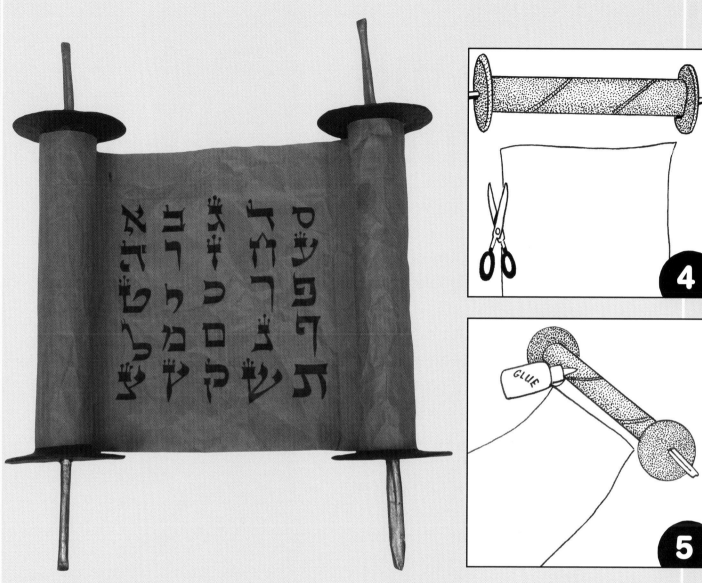

## Step 5

Glue or tape the ends of the paper to the cardboard tubes, as shown. Roll each side until you expose just enough paper to write on.

## Step 6

Using scrap paper, practice some examples of ancient Hebrew characters or letters, such as the ones shown here. Then carefully draw pencil lines on your scroll before completing your favorite Hebrew passage or the basic Hebrew alphabet, as shown. Color in the pencil-drawn characters with black paint or markers.

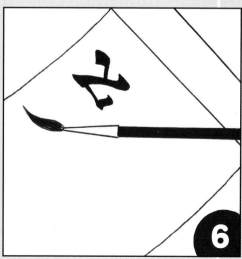

# Rituals and Celebrations

The Hebrews were monotheists (people who worship only one god), while those living among them were very much opposed to the idea of a single god. The Romans, Greeks, and Egyptians were all pagans and believed in the worship of many gods. Occasionally, however, during times of greater mixing of cultures, such as during the Hellenistic period, members of pagan communities who came into contact with the Hebrews would convert to Judaism.

Judaism, like most religions, includes rituals and celebrations that serve to honor certain important historical and spiritual events. Some days of the year are set aside to reflect upon one's actions in the previous year, such as the Day of Atonement (Yom Kippur), while the Festival of Booths (Sukkot) celebrates life and the fall harvest.

One of the most well-known Jewish celebrations is Hanukkah, a joyous festival that commemorates the end of Syrian occupation of Israel and the rededication of the temple in

*A man marks doorposts with lamb's blood so the Angel of Death will pass over his home on the night of the final plague in Egypt. This event is commemorated during the Jewish holiday of Passover.*

Jerusalem (164 BC). In order to perform the necessary ritual to rededicate the temple to God, an oil lamp needed to be lit and could not then be extinguished (representing eternal light).

Yet, only enough oil for one day was on hand. Miraculously, the small supply of oil lasted for eight days. During Hanukkah, Jews re-create this "mystery of lights" by lighting one candle on a menorah (an eight-candle candelabra) every night for an eight-day period. The ninth and center candle is lit every night, and its flame is used to light the others.

The most widely observed Jewish holiday is Passover, which has its origins in the Hebrews' exodus from Egypt. Before God unleashed the final plague on the Egyptians—the death of every firstborn son in Egypt—it was said that Moses had the Israelites swab lamb's blood on their doors as a way of letting the Angel of Death know that those were the homes of Jews; the Angel would then pass over those houses and spare the firstborn sons who lived there. Jews eat matzo (a flat bread containing no yeast) during Passover because the Israelites left Egypt so quickly they did not have time to allow their bread to finish rising. Other foods eaten during Passover include horseradish, which symbolizes the bitterness felt by the Jews for having been enslaved, and a mixture of crushed nuts and apples, representing the bricks of mortar and straw that Hebrew slaves were forced to make in Egypt.

*This seder plate contains the foods eaten during Passover. Each item represents an aspect of Hebrew captivity in Egypt.*

*Menorahs are among the oldest symbols of the Jewish faith. Seven-branched candelabras, like the one below, were used in Solomon's Temple. A Hanukkah menorah has nine branches and commemorates the eight-day "mystery of lights."*

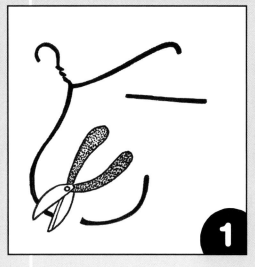

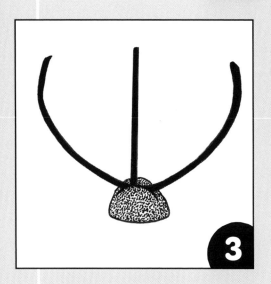

# Menorah *

*Before the menorah was included as part of the Hanukkah celebration, it was a religious symbol that decorated ancient synagogues.*

* ADULT SUPERVISION IS REQUIRED FOR THIS CRAFT.

### YOU WILL NEED
- Wire hanger
- Wire cutter
- Oven-baking polymer clay
- Craft paint
- Glass or ceramic baking dish

### Step 1
Have an adult help you cut a wire hanger to make the basic form of the menorah. Starting with the smallest pieces first, cut two pieces of wire, each approximately 7 inches long. Bend one of the pieces into an arch, as shown.

### Step 2
Cut the next piece of wire approximately 10 inches long. Cut the last one approximately 12 inches long. Bend these two wires into an arch, just as you did with the first length of wire.

### Step 3
Roll a lump of clay into a large ball, suitable for the menorah base. Flatten the bottom of the ball and stick the straight wire into the center. Press the largest arched wire into the clay, as shown.

### Step 4
Roll small balls of clay and bead them onto the arched wire, securing it to the base. Add two clay "beads" to the straight wire before placing the next arched wire. Lay the base flat while you build the menorah's "branches."

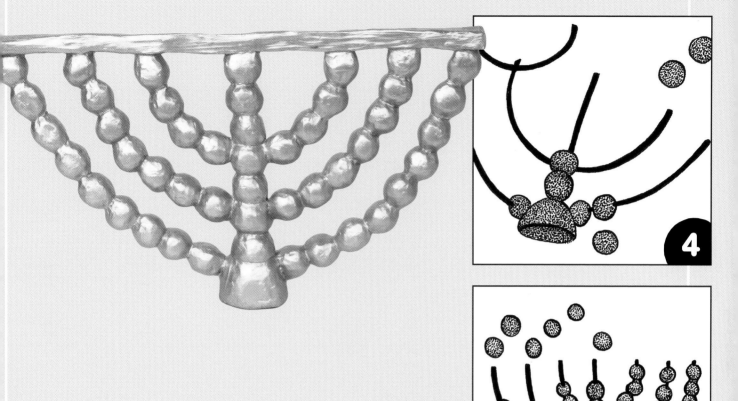

## Step 5

Repeat the method used in step 4 to attach all the wire branches of the menorah. Once the form is in place, bead the remaining exposed wire areas with clay balls.

## Step 6

Roll a long tube of clay and flatten its sides. Attach it to the top of your menorah. Join all of the clay balls together by blending the clay with a toothpick. When you are finished joining the balls on this side, carefully turn the menorah over and secure the balls on the reverse side. When you are finished, have an adult help you bake the clay, following the package instructions. After the menorah has cooled, paint it with bronze or gold craft paint.

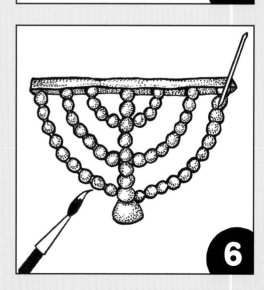

# Clothing

The ancient Israelites based many clothing decisions upon Jewish law, or the Torah, and their religious commitments guided every aspect of their lifestyle, determining the way they worked, played, prayed, ate, and drank.

Because the Scriptures encouraged a modest, unadorned appearance, the attire of the Hebrews was often very simple. But it could be embellished in various creative ways, depending on the circumstances and one's social standing. The clothing of the high priests and nobility was often colorfully embroidered with trims and small braids and adorned with tassels and tiny bells. These embellishments, in addition to being decorative, were also meant to act as a memory device for their wearers, reminding them of God's commandments.

Men usually dressed in a long, shirtlike garment, similar in style to a

*Prayer shawls reflect God's command to the Israelites to wear fringes and tassels on the corners of their garments.*

Roman tunic but much simpler. This garment was usually tied around the waist. Men also wore beards with a longer lock of hair on each side of their face called a *pe'ot*. They covered their heads with close-fitting caps. Because of Jewish law, Israelites could wear linen or wool clothing, but not a combination of both.

Women dressed in a simple, modest fashion. Women covered their heads with a shawl or similar piece of fabric. Israelite women enjoyed wearing perfume and cosmetics, probably influenced by the Egyptians of the same time period who commonly indulged in many different types of scents, oils, facial powders, eye makeup, and even wigs. Archaeologists have found some evidence of traditional Hebrew women's artifacts, such as makeup palettes that were used to grind various natural materials together to create colored pigments.

Many women also enjoyed simple gold jewelry such as earrings, but the Hebrews were not well known for their metalworking abilities. Most of these objects were owned by the wealthy and may have been imported from other places such as Greece. Most jewelry worn by Israelites was made from clay, a readily available material throughout the entire Mediterranean area.

Both sandals and shoes were worn in ancient Israel. Sandals were worn by nearly everyone since they were inexpensive to make. Their soles were made of wood or animal hides and were fastened with leather straps. Indoors, most people went barefoot after washing their feet upon entering a building. Wealthier Hebrews wore closed-toed shoes, which were often decorated lavishly.

*These mirrors and jewelry box were found in the Cave of Letters in the Judean desert of eastern Israel.*

*These are a young woman's sandals found in Judean desert caves.*

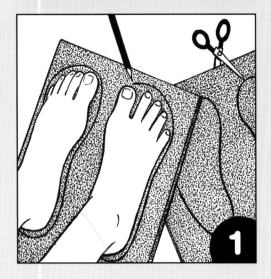

# Hebrew Sandals

*Find an extra long shirt, grab a scarf or necktie to wrap around your waist, and then slip on these cardboard sandals to complete your ancient costume.*

### YOU WILL NEED
- Cardboard
- String or twine
- Scissors
- Pencil or pen
- Masking tape
- Craft paint

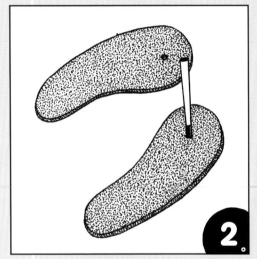

### Step 1
Trace the outline of each foot twice onto a piece of cardboard. Cut out the four shapes using your scissors. These will form the soles and insoles of your sandals.

### Step 2
Place your feet onto one pair of cutout soles and mark the area between your big and second toe with a small mark. Remove your feet and carefully puncture with the tip of your scissors a hole through each sole at the mark you made. Paint this set of soles (the insoles) with craft paint, if you desire. Set them aside to dry.

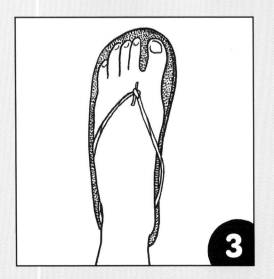

### Step 3
There are many different materials you can use to turn these cardboard shapes into sandals. You can use twine, ribbon, yarn, or strips of fabric. (We used braided string.) Take a long piece of string and loosely wrap it around the heel to the middle of your foot, as shown. Tie it into a knot to form a band around your foot.

### Step 4
Take another long piece of string and tie one end to the knot of the band. Insert the other end through the hole in the cardboard. With the band around your foot, and

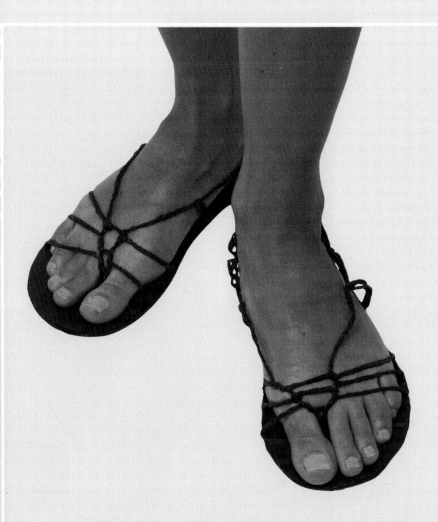

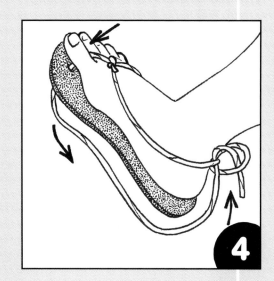

the new piece between your toe, thread the string along the bottom of the sole and up to the heel. Tie it to the band. Run a long piece of tape along the bottom of the insoles to secure the string.

## Step 5

Knot another piece of string to the band at the arch of your foot. Bring the string around the bottom and up to the opposite side of the band. Tie the string in place and tape it under the insole. Repeat this step, tie, and tape additional string along the band to the heel.

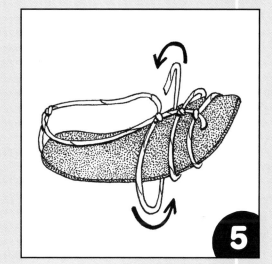

## Step 6

Glue the bottom of the insoles to the other set of cardboard soles, making sure to cover the entire bottom of the insoles with glue to ensure that the shapes stick together securely.

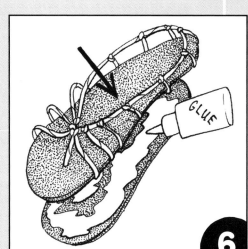

# Hebrew Potters

**M**uch can be learned about the history of the ancient Hebrews by examining what remains of their pottery. These earthenware designs varied greatly depending on when they were made and their place of origin. Major stages of Hebrew history may be identified by their particular choice of pottery shape, the type of clay that was used, and the styles of the pieces' painted designs. In fact, pottery styles tell archaeologists and historians a great deal about how the Hebrews traveled and traded throughout the Mediterranean area.

Pottery was an essential item for every Hebrew family, especially because the Israelites were often transient and needed to transport large quantities of food supplies. Some clay artifacts discovered by archaeologists have included kitchen utensils, large jars that were used for carrying oil, the lamps that held the oil (which were no more elaborate than small clay bowls), and vessels for wine, water, and food.

*These are replicas of storage pots found in an underground olive oil storage room.*

Most ordinary pottery was made of brown or gray earthenware, shaped by hand using the coil method (rings of clay stacked on top of one another and then smoothed) or on a primitive potter's wheel. Decorative items such as jewelry were polished, painted, or engraved before being fired (baked).

The use of pottery was so widespread that all sorts of objects were stored in earthenware containers; for example, it was common for ancient scrolls to be stored in tall clay vessels, such as the ones in which the Dead Sea Scrolls were found.

*This burnished clay jug hails from the early Roman period of Israel's history, around the first century BC.*

Because pottery was so commonly used, it is safe to say that most men, and probably women, too, knew a great deal about how to handle clay. Ancient texts explain that the Hebrew people mixed the wet clay with sand or fine quartz, straw, or goat's hair before working it by hand or on a wheel. Adding this texture helped the clay keep its shape and prevented breaking while it hardened.

Some of the most interesting clay pieces to emerge from the hands of Hebrew craftspeople are multiwicked oil lamps. These lamps produced more light than the common single-wick lamps, but they required more care and attention when burning. They were probably used in public places where greater light was needed.

*This is an eight wick oil lamp.*

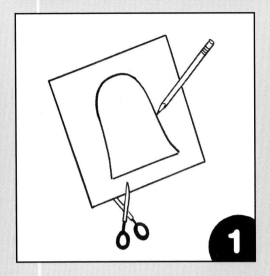

# Oil Lamp

*Brighten the dark, long nights of winter by constructing this model of an ancient Hebrew oil lamp.*

### YOU WILL NEED
- Air-drying terra-cotta clay
- Paper and pencil
- Scissors
- Non-serrated knife
- Assorted clay tools or common kitchen utensils

### Step 1
Draw the shape you would like for the base of your oil lamp on a piece of paper. A simple shape of an arched line with a straight bottom will do. Cut out the shape and set aside. This will be your stencil.

### Step 2
Roll two large handfuls of clay into flat patties with a half-inch thickness. One patty should be slightly larger around than the other. Trace the stencil shape onto both clay pieces and cut them out with a knife.

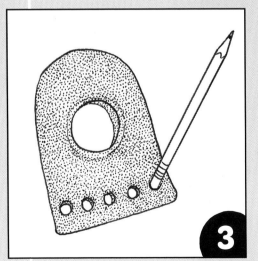

### Step 3
Cut a circular hole in the center of the larger patty. Make holes along the bottom using the eraser end of a pencil. This is the top half of the oil lamp.

### Step 4
Fit the top half over the second clay shape you cut in step 2 by bending the top piece into an arch.

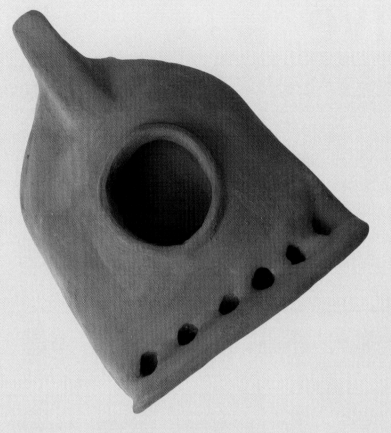

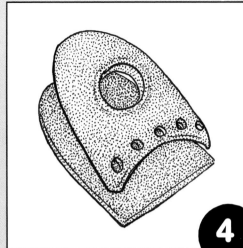

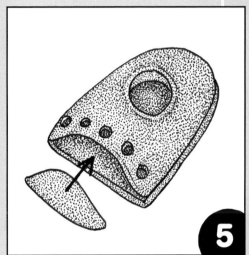

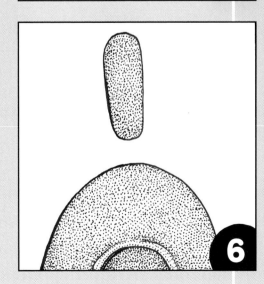

## Step 5
Roll a small piece of clay to fit on the open end along the bottom. Blend the clay along the sides of both halves and the bottom to secure the form.

## Step 6
Add a handle by attaching a small piece of rolled clay. Once you are satisfied with your design, allow it to fully dry. Since this is only a decorative model of an oil lamp, do not try to light it by adding wicks or oil.

# Decorative Arts

Although the Hebrews were often uprooted from their homeland and forced to live either in captivity or in wandering exile, they were still able to express themselves through art like most ancient, and more stable and settled, civilizations did, often adopting the artistic skills of the Greeks and the Egyptians. In addition to homegrown art, many Israelites also traded goods, gaining beautiful jewelry and other decorative objects in the process. Wealthier Israelites simply hired foreign artisans to beautify their homes.

One of the most common and readily available ways for wealthy Hebrews to express their love for both art and religion was through dress. Hebrew spinners and weavers were every bit as accomplished at cloth production, dyeing, and patterning as their Egyptian counterparts, as the few surviving swatches of cloth attest.

The Hebrews, like other civilizations of the day, had sophisticated methods for dyeing cloth and preferred colorful clothes. One color that

*This ancient floor mosaic from a synagogue in Naaran, Israel, depicts a Torah tabernacle covered by a curtain.*

common people were forbidden to use, however, was purple, because the substance required to make purple dye—the blood of certain shellfish—was so rare. This is why the color was long associated with royalty. Other rare colors included scarlet and crimson and were obtained from the eggs of certain insects found only in a specific kind of oak tree. These colors were reserved for the garments of priests and royalty and were worn only on specific, solemn occasions.

Jewelry is frequently mentioned in the Hebrew Bible. Bracelets were often the insignia of kings and priests, who also wore richly decorated accessories. The high priest (*Kohen Gadol*), for example, wore a breastplate that was embedded with twelve different gems—each representing one of the tribes of Israel— and set in gold filigree. A diadem—a pure gold plate—was set in his turban, and his shoulders were adorned with two precious stones set in gold.

In addition to the special clothing, jewelry, and accessories worn by the nobility and priests, pottery, bone and ivory objects, amulets, silver scrolls, and glass bottles have been discovered in burial tombs in the Hinnom Valley, southwest of Jerusalem. Limited by their often nomadic existence and turbulent foreign occupations, the ancient Israelites have nevertheless left us some stunning examples of their artistry.

*A Jewish high priest wears a breastplate with twelve gems, each representing one of the original tribes of Israel.*

*This ancient jewelry hails from Caesaria.*

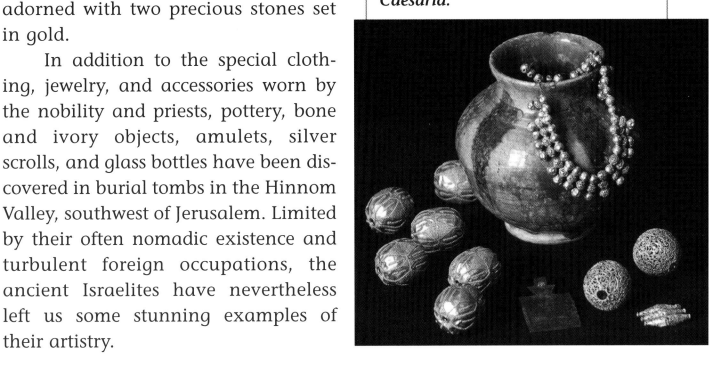

# Beaded Jewelry

*Create the most common type of ancient Hebrew jewelry: clay beads.*

### YOU WILL NEED

- Salt clay
- String
- Toothpicks
- Pencil
- Craft paint
- Paintbrush

*Salt Clay Recipe*

2 cups salt
1 cup cornstarch
1 cup water

*Mix 2 cups of salt with 1 cup of cornstarch in a saucepan. Add 1 cup of water and stir the ingredients thoroughly. Heat over a low flame for about five minutes, constantly stirring until the mixture becomes thick and pastelike. Remove the clay from the pan and place it to cool on a baking sheet for about twenty-five minutes.*

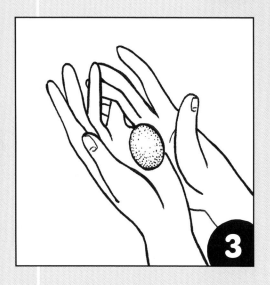

### Step 1
Make the salt clay using the recipe on this page.

### Step 2
Roll a long length of the clay on a table, cutting even lengths every inch or so. These will become your beads, so make the lengths as equal as possible.

### Step 3
Take each separate inch of salt clay and roll it in the palm of your hand until smooth.

### Step 4
When you are satisfied with its size, make tiny designs in the clay with a toothpick, or roll the bead on something that has a texture, like a rock, the spiral edge of a notebook, or a basket with a woven design. Almost any textured surface will do. Experiment until you gain the effect you desire.

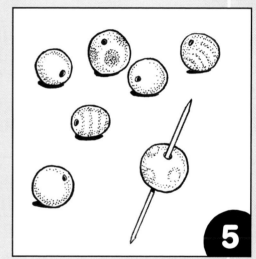

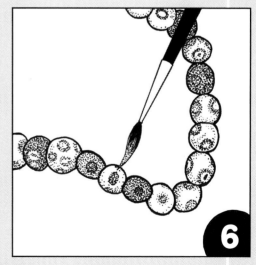

## Step 5
Repeat steps 3 and 4 until you have enough beads for a necklace. With a toothpick, pierce each bead through the middle so you can thread it later. Set all the beads aside to dry.

## Step 6
When the beads are dry, paint them with different colored craft paints. After the paint dries, you can string the beads into beautiful necklaces or bracelets.

# Art and Leisure

T he ancient Israelites were fond of dancing and music when they were not at work farming or doing other hard labor. Usually, dancing, music, and other recreational activities were a way of worshiping and giving thanks to God. King David is said to have led people in celebrations of thanksgiving that featured singing and dancing following victories in battle. Before he became king of Israel, he served King Saul as the court harpist.

*In this painting, David plays the harp before Saul.*

Archaeologists have found the remains of many musical instruments that would have been played during religious celebrations and royal entertainments, including the shofar, a ram's horn trumpet. It is the only traditional instrument still used in Jewish ceremonies today. Its primitive, primal tones were thought to possess supernatural powers. Examples of the kinds of songs the ancient Hebrews sang during religious ceremonies are contained within the Bible in the Book of Psalms, many of which are traditionally thought to have been written by David. In some of the Old Testament scrolls, small markings can be seen above the text of the psalms, an early system of musical notation.

There is also a great deal of evidence to indicate that the Hebrews played games, including many board games with dice and game pieces. These activities were portable and were probably enjoyed by children and adults of all ages. Upon arriving in Canaan, the Hebrews may have encountered games played by their Canaanite neighbors. One of these may have been called the "game of fifty-eight holes." With a board commonly carved out of ivory, this was a game that was played with dice and moveable pegs that each player moved around the board. A similar game was called the "game of twenty squares."

*wooden dreidels*

*This is a replica of a biblical harp.*

One of the most famous Hebrew games is played with the dreidel, a four-sided top that is spun. Depending on which of four Hebrew characters is on top when the dreidel stops spinning, the player loses or wins candy (or nuts, coins, beads, and marbles). The game may have its origins in a sad period of Jewish history. Some claim that when the Syrians outlawed the study of the Torah during their occupation of Israel in the second century BC, Jews would keep a dreidel on the table while they were studying. That way, if Syrian soldiers walked by, they could hide their books and pretend to be playing a game.

*This thirteenth century BC Canaanite gaming board is made of ivory inlaid with gold and blue paste.*

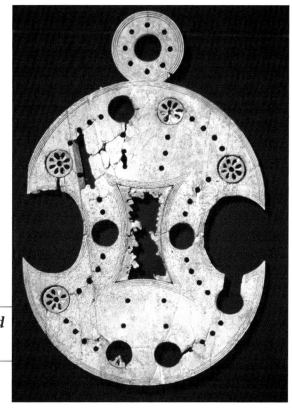

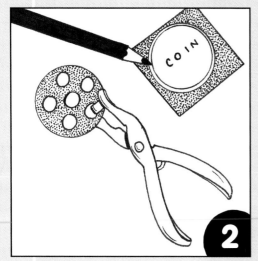

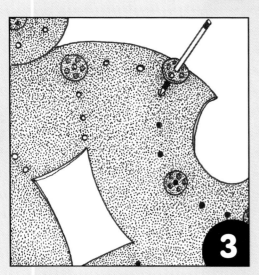

# Game Board ✡

*Use your imagination and create your own game to play on this ancient Canaanite game board.*

\* ADULT SUPERVISION IS REQUIRED FOR THIS CRAFT.

### YOU WILL NEED
• Large cardboard box
• Coffee can and a quarter
• Pen and pencil
• Scissors
• Craft knife
• Hole puncher
• Tacky glue
• Four paper cups
• Clay (see salt clay recipe on page 38)
• Craft paint
• String

### Step 1
Draw a large oval on a piece of heavy cardboard. Using the bottom of the can, trace a circle at the top of the oval. Trace the rim of your paper cup to make half circles at the left and right side of the oval, as shown. Cut out your shape, but cut the cup half circles slightly smaller than the traced line.

### Step 2
Trace a quarter onto a piece of cardboard. Make roughly ten or eleven circles. Cut them out. Using a hole puncher, make a hole in the center of each circle. Punch holes around the center hole as well. These discs will act as bases on the board.

### Step 3
Set the cardboard coins onto the board and mark the center hole of each one. Make dots along the game board approximately 1/2 inch apart. Carefully puncture these dots to make holes using the tip of a ballpoint pen.

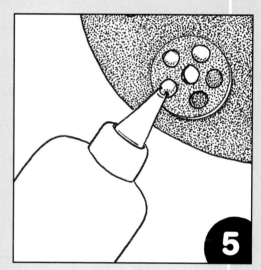

## Step 4

Glue the rim of two paper cups to the bottom of the board where the side openings are. These will hold the game pieces. Glue the bottoms of two additional cups to the top and bottom of the game board. Make a line of glue around the edge of the center rectangle and glue a scrap piece of cardboard to it. Allow the glue to dry before turning the board over. When dry, glue the coins from step 2 onto the topside, over the punctured holes.

## Step 5

Apply glue to string around the edge of the board. To make a dice well, trace a rectangle in the board's center with glue and cover it with string. You can fill the decorative holes on your bases with tacky glue, making a paste inlay. When your board is dry, paint it as desired.

## Step 6

Using the salt clay recipe on page 38, make small balls of clay. Flatten the sides of two of the balls to make dice. To make pegs, take small, rolled tubes of clay and pinch one end into a point. Allow the clay to dry before playing. Paint the dice and pegs, if you desire.

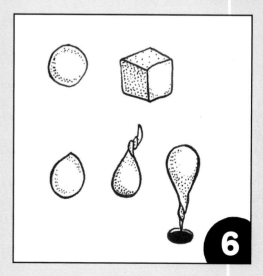

# TIMELINE

| | | |
|---|---|---|
| BC | **3500** | Egyptians develop first hieroglyphs. |
| | **2575** | Egypt's Old Kingdom begins. Great Pyramids and the Sphinx in Giza are started. |
| | **1730** | Hyksos invades Egypt and the Israelites settle there. |
| | **1567** | New Kingdom begins in Egypt. |
| | **1333** | Tutankhamen rules over Egypt and brings back the worship of many gods. |
| | **1304** | King Ramses II rules over Egypt. |
| | **1270** | Israelites leave Egypt. |
| | **1163** | King Ramses III, the last great pharaoh of Egypt, dies. |
| | **1004** | David becomes king of Israel. |
| | **965** | King David dies. |
| | **922** | Israel splits into Israel and Judah. |
| | **722** | Israel is conquered by Assyria, and the Hebrews are exiled to Babylon. |
| | **539** | Persian King Cyrus defeats Babylonia and helps the Israelites rebuild the temple in Jerusalem. |
| | **336** | Alexander the Great rules Greece. |
| | **147** | Rome rules over Greece. |
| | **63** | Rome occupies Israel. |
| | **49** | Julius Caesar rules Rome. |
| | **30** | Egypt becomes a Roman province. |
| **AD** | **5** | Approximate birth of Jesus in Bethlehem. |
| | **43** | Romans invade Britain. |
| | **54** | Nero becomes Rome's emperor and outlaws Christianity. |
| | **70** | Romans destroy Jerusalem. Jews disperse to surrounding cities. |
| | **117** | Roman Empire is at its greatest point. |
| | **138** | Plague, war, and famine create unrest in Roman cities. |
| | **286** | Roman Empire is divided. |
| | **1948** | The modern nation of Israel is founded. |

# GLOSSARY

**Canaan**  The land along the Mediterranean Sea said to have been promised to the Hebrews by God.

**Diaspora**  Greek word for dispersion; the scattering of Jews from their homeland to many other nations.

**exile**  To be banished or sent away from one's own home.

**exodus**  Ancient Hebrews' flight from slavery in Egypt.

**Hellenistic**  Time in which the Greek culture was at an intellectual and creative high point.

**idol**  An image or statue that is worshiped; a false god.

**Judaism**  Jewish belief system.

**menorah**  Ancient seven-branched oil-burning candle that was placed in Solomon's Temple. Today, menorahs are nine-branched candelabras that are lit over eight nights of Hanukkah to commemorate the "mystery of lights."

**monotheism**  Belief in only one god.

**nomadic**  People or tribe that has no permanent place and moves from area to area.

**pagan**  Person who believes in many gods.

**papyrus**  Form of paper made from a reedy water plant that grew along the Nile River in Egypt.

**parchment**  The skin of a sheep or goat prepared in such a way that one could write on it, as if on paper.

**plague**  Outbreak of disease or other calamity.

**Promised Land**  Area promised to the Hebrew people by God, located in southern Canaan.

**scribes**  Literate men who would draw up contracts, keep accounts, and maintain records.

**Septuagint**  Greek translation of the Hebrew Bible.

**shofar**  Ram's horn trumpet.

**shoftim**  Leaders or uncrowned kings of the twelve tribes of Israel.

**stylus**  Pointed or wedge-shaped stick used for making impressions on wet clay tablets.

**Tanakh**  Hebrew Bible consisting of the Torah, books of the prophets, and other sacred writings.

**Torah**  The five books of Moses that were delivered by   on top of Mount Sinai.

**zealot**  An Israelite violently opposed to the Roman occupation of Israel.

# FOR MORE INFORMATION

## ORGANIZATIONS

**Archaeological Institute of America**
656 Beacon Street, 4th Floor
Boston, MA 02215-20006
(617) 353-9361
Web site: http://www.archaeology.org

**Metropolitan Museum of Art**
1000 Fifth Avenue
New York, NY 10028-0198
(212) 535-7710
Web site: http://www.metmuseum.org

**Smithsonian Institution Information Center**
1000 Jefferson Drive SW
Washington, DC 20560-0010
(202) 357-2700
Web site: http://www.si.edu

**World Archaeological Society**
120 Lakewood Drive
Hollister, MO 65672
(417) 334-2377

## In Canada

**Ontario Archaeological Society**
11099 Bathurst Street
Richmond Hill, ON L4C 0N2
(905) 787-9851
Web site: http://www.ontarioarchaeology.
on.ca

## WEB SITES

**Ancient Canaan**
http://www.penncharter.com/student/
israel/index.html

**Dig! The Archaeology Magazine for Kids**
http://www.digonsite.com

**Echoes from the Ancients**
http://www.pbs.org/echoes

**Internet Jewish History Sourcebook**
http://www.fordham.edu/halsall/jewish/
jewishsbook.html

## FOR FURTHER READING

Brinkley, Joel, ed. *Israel: The Historical Atlas.* New York: Hungry Minds, Inc., 1997.

Isserlin, B. S. J. *The Israelites.* London, UK: Thames and Hudson, 1998.

Mann, Kenny. *The Ancient Hebrews.* Tarrytown, NY: Marshall Cavendish, 1999.

Mendenhall, George E. *Ancient Israel's Faith and History: An Introduction to the Bible in Context.* Louisville, KY: Westminster John Knox Press, 2001.

Merrill, Eugene H. *Kingdom of Priests: A History of the Old Testament Israel.* Grand Rapids, MI: Baker Book House, 1997.

# INDEX

## A
Abraham, 4–5
Alexandria, 11
Arabic, 11, 20
Aramaic, 11, 20
Ark of the Covenant, 7, 12, 13, 16, 17

## B
Babylonians, 7, 8, 11, 12, 17
Bible, 4, 17
biblical history, 4

## C
Canaan, 4–5, 7, 12, 33
classical Hebrew, 10
Cyrus, 8

## D
David, 7, 12, 40
Dead Sea Scrolls, 20–21, 33
Diaspora, 7

## E
Egyptians, 5–6, 7, 20, 29, 36
exodus, 5, 6

## G
Greeks, 7, 8, 11, 20, 36

## H
Hanukkah, 24–25
Hebrews
    art of, 11, 12–13, 36–37, 40–41
    and the Babylonians, 7, 8, 11, 12, 17
    Bible of, 5, 10, 11, 20
    clothing of, 28–29, 37
    daily life of, 9–10
    education and, 10
    and the Egyptians, 5–6, 7, 10
    exodus of, 5
    family life of, 10
    games of, 41
    and the Greeks, 7, 8, 11
    history of, 4–9
    languages of, 10–11, 21
    religion of, 16–17, 24
    rituals of, 24–25
    and the Romans, 8–9, 10
Hellenistic period, 8, 11, 24
Hyksos, 5

## I
Israel, 4, 5, 7, 8, 9, 24
    twelve tribes of, 7
Israelites, 4, 5, 6, 7, 28

## J
Jesus, 8
Joshua, 7
Judah, 7, 8
Judaism, 24
Judea, 8, 9

## M
menorah, 25
Mesopotamia, 4, 7
Mishnaic Hebrew, 10–11
modern Hebrew, 11
Moses, 6–7

## N
Nebuchadnezzar, 7
nomads, 4, 9

## P
pagans, 24
Palestine, 9
Passover, 25
pe'ot, 28
Persia, 8
pharaohs, 5, 6
Philistines, 7
plagues, 6

## Q
Qumran, 21

## R
Rabbinic Hebrew, 10–11
Ramses II, 5
Romans, 8–9, 11

## S
Saul, 40
scribes, 10
Septuagint, 11
shofar, 40
shoftim, 7
Solomon, 7, 12
Solomon's Temple, 7, 12, 16
Sukkot, 24

## T
Tanakh, 11
Ten Commandments, 6, 7, 16
Torah, 6

## Y
Yiddish, 20
Yom Kippur, 16, 24

## ABOUT THE AUTHOR AND ILLUSTRATOR

Joann Jovinelly and Jason Netelkos have been working together on one project or another for more than a decade. This is their first collaborative series for young readers. They live in New York City.

## PHOTO CREDITS

Cover artifact, p. 25 (bottom) © Réunion des Musées Nationaus/Art Resource, NY; pp. 4, 21 (middle), 29 (top) © Granger Collection, New York; pp. 5, 6, 8, 12, 17 (top), 37 (top) © North Wind Pictures; p. 9 © Scala/Art Resource, NY; p. 10 © ASAP Ltd./Index Stock Imagery, Inc.; p. 13 (top) © Pictor; pp. 13 (bottom), 20 © Richard T. Nowitz/Corbis; pp. 16, 17 (bottom), 21 (top and bottom), p. 25 (top) © SuperStock; p. 24 © The Jewish Museum, New York/SuperStock; p. 28 © Coxe-Goldberg Photography/Art Resource; p. 29 (bottom) © Reuben and Edith Hecht Museum, University of Haifa; pp. 32, 41 (middle) © Richard T. Nowitz/Corbis; pp. 33 (top and bottom), 40, 41 (top) © The Jewish Museum, New York/Art Resource; p. 36 © Erich Lessing/Art Resource, NY; p. 37 (bottom) © David Rubinger/Corbis; p. 41 (bottom) courtesy of the Oriental Institute of the University of Chicago. All craft illustrations and crafts by Jason Netelkos; all craft photographs by Adriana Skura.

## SERIES DESIGN AND LAYOUT

Evelyn Horovicz

## ACKNOWLEDGMENTS

Special thanks to Nicole Netelkos-Goetchius for her continued support.